What Comes First?

A BOOK ABOUT SEQUENCES

BY NICK REBMAN

Published by The Child's World®
1980 Lookout Drive • Mankato, MN 56003-1705
800-599-READ • www.childsworld.com

Acknowledgments
The Child's World®: Mary Swensen, Publishing Director
Red Line Editorial: Editorial direction and production
The Design Lab: Design

Photographs ©: Design Lab, cover; bdspn/iStockphoto/
Thinkstock, 4; Fuse/Thinkstock, 5; Purestock/Thinkstock, 6;
Monkey Business Images/Thinkstock, 7; Wojciech Gajda/
iStockphoto/Thinkstock, 8; David De Lossy/Photodisc/
Thinkstock, 9; iStockphoto, 10, 11; Monkey Business Images/
iStockphoto, 12; Wavebreakmedia/iStockphoto, 13

ISBN 9781503807631
LCCN 2015958225

Printed in the United States of America
Mankato, MN
June, 2016
PA02306

About the Author

Nick Rebman likes to write, draw, and travel. He lives in Minnesota.

Some things happen first. Some things happen last. Can you answer these questions about when things happen?

Maya likes her garden. She puts a seed in the ground. Weeks later there is a plant in her garden.

What comes first?

When Luke was a baby, he liked to crawl. Now Luke is a kid who likes to play baseball.

What does he
do first?

Abby is tired. She brushes her teeth.
She gets into bed and closes her eyes.

What comes last?

Jack goes outside in the snow. He starts building a snowman. He puts a hat and scarf on his snowman.

What comes last?

Zoe and her dad go to the grocery store. They buy lots of food. They go home and cook a meal.

What comes first?

13

ANSWER KEY

Maya puts the seed in the ground first.

Luke crawls first.

Abby closes her eyes last.

Jack puts a hat and scarf on his snowman last.

Zoe and her dad go to the grocery store first.

GLOSSARY

first (FURST) The thing that is first comes before everything else. Maya put the seed in the ground first. Luke crawled first. Zoe and her dad went to the grocery store first.

last (LAST) The thing that is last comes after everything else. Abby closed her eyes last. Jake put clothes on his snowman last.

TO LEARN MORE

IN THE LIBRARY

Basic Beginnings: Counting and Sequencing. Greensboro,
NC: Carson-Dellosa Publishing Group, 2012.

Patterns and Sequencing. Westminster, CA: Teacher Created Resources, 2007.

Sequencing and Memory Workbook. Greensboro, NC:
Carson-Dellosa Publishing Group, 2015.

ON THE WEB

Visit our Web site for links about sequences: **childsworld.com/links**

Note to Parents, Teachers, and Librarians: We routinely verify our Web links to make
sure they are safe and active sites. So encourage your readers to check them out!

INDEX